Poetry
To Ponder

Poetry
To Ponder

ANDY HAWK

XULON PRESS

Xulon Press
2301 Lucien Way #415
Maitland, FL 32751
407.339.4217
www.xulonpress.com

Paperback ISBN-13: 978-1-6628-0156-3

Ebook ISBN-13: 978-1-6628-0157-0

Contents

Introduction

Reading poetry can be enjoyable in itself, but its true entertainment lies in how it is thought about after it is read. Imagery and phrases that stood out can be pleasantly meditated on. If a rhythm bobbed along with an amusing cadence, if word groupings interested us in a personal way, or if an antithetical question gave us pause, the entire poem seems to be worthwhile.

If it prompted us in some way to enjoy thinking about it, it became a vehicle for allowing us to entertain ourselves by letting our minds dwell on it.

Most of what is read in a given day has specific purposes and applications. An assembly manual tells how to put a barbecue grill together. Spreadsheets are studied to perform functions of work. Texting might be fun, but most messages are viewed to see if some kind of action is required from the person who received it. Reading novels is a wonderful hobby but requires diligence to follow a formulaic narrative structure. Poetry is different. It doesn't beg to be understood completely, demand its principles be agreed with and adhered to, or feel slighted if it's not liked. It is often a short piece, told in increments, with an opportunity to be engaged with it and be impacted by it on whatever level it was meaningful.

Any philosophical meaning is presented as an artistic demonstration, not an all-conclusive argument for it or empirical definition of it. Poetry offers respite the same way song lyrics do.

It is written to fall into a category separate from everything else. It wants the reader to think and feel something from it.

The poems of *Poetry to Ponder* were included with this in mind. All of them have been publicly read or shared, and feedback has been noted. Questions of content or suggestions to improve were fielded, but markers of approval have centered on how the poems resonated with people individually. There was agreement on some things that were commonly liked, but most people enjoyed different aspects of a particular poem and had favorite parts that were personal to them. Sharing of ideas was invigorating for everyone. Reading the poems was rewarding, but whatever thoughts and feelings that were evoked and discussed brought even more entertainment to it. Thinking about a poem connected us to it, and sharing ideas about it connected us to each other. Some of the poems I have written didn't achieve that; *Poetry to Ponder* is a compilation of the poems that did.

To facilitate entertainment through a thinking and sharing dynamic, I have included a two-part exercise to engage readers more closely with the poems. This can be informally done and should not serve as a rubric to determine whether a poem is good or not. The first component is a critical exercise to give an overall impression of a poem for its title, rhyme, word usage, meter, length, and theme. The second component is a creative exercise where the readers clearly identify what is liked or disliked or is clear or unclear and is given the opportunity to express how they would alter the poem if they wanted to. The discussion of opinions should become much more lively using the two exercises as guidelines.

My greatest hope is that those who chose to read, think, and discuss *Poetry to Ponder* would find it to be a great addition to what they already enjoy reading and that they would value the poems not for the writings themselves but the entertainment thinking about them inspires.

Critical And Creative Exercises

1. Critique the poem regarding the following criteria:

    a. title

    b. meter

    c. rhyme

    d. length

    e. theme

    f. word usage

2. Creative activity. You may wish to do this on a separate piece of paper.

    a. Circle phrases and words that are liked or meaningful.

    b. Draw a line through words or phrases that are not liked.

c. Put question marks next to words or phrases that are unclear.

d. If part of the poem would be more suitable in another place, put put parentheses around it and draw arrows to where you would like for it to be moved.

e. Change the title.

f. Change the ending.

g. Alter any word usage or punctuation.

h. Recite the poem using any particular voice or accent you wish.

The Song He Sang And The Song I Heard

Oh, bird on barren branch,
have you a song?
have you my song?
with words I know and those I forgot?

is today too late to sing it?
is tomorrow too late to hear it?
is patience measured by the drag of a day
or in the mereness of a minute?
and how long should I think about it?

The bird chirped and flew away,
but oh, that single chirp!
in it
I heard:
distant church bells through dark night rain,
the bearded whistle of a man in a cornfield,
an oar dripping off the side of a boat,

a horse's hoof on cobblestone,
a piano tune that finds lost tears,
the closing of a finished book,
serving spoons in Thanksgiving bowls,
the applause of a winning score,
a barber's snip,
a grandfather clock,
the footsteps of a pet,
the bite of a peach,
the sleepy breath of a child,
and the words "I love you"
from the one person
you needed to hear it from the most;

Yes, he was gone,
and winter was still here;
his song was over,
but mine continued,
and I wouldn't have known my song
without his.

Still

the open eye sees that it's gone,
the closed eye looks for it,
and the heart reveals it to both;

and even though we know where it is,
the ache of missing it
hurts worse than we thought it would;

if it's safe,
we still long to protect it;
if it's happy,
we still wish to smile with it;
and if we dance,
we pretend it's there with us
for no one ever dances alone;

the soul says,
"unearth it from me
for it is not dead

3

and never will be as long as you remember it;"

the heart says,
"rejoice with me in sadness
for shared value has no greater worth;"

and the open eye
and the closed eye
both weep;
for although one looks out
and the other looks in,
they both see the same thing;
and where they both meet,
the happiness of what was
still is.

Heavendale

It is in the hills of Heavendale,
where birds and rain sing the same song,
and the sun and the moon both love you;

It is where the wind on your face
reminds you
that you are never alone,
and if it leaves,
it will faithfully return;

distant lightning gives hope,
and soft thunder understands your secrets;

and when sluggish flies turn black,
misery will soon die with them,
and next year,
their brief return
means they will simply die again;

a cycle of peace,
turning with the wheels of seasons,
finds Heavendale again,
and it embraces you,
just like it has before.

A Balloon Passes By

a red balloon
it's round, it's red
it's round, it's red, it's round;

floats on by
up high in sky
up high, on by, in sky;

look down at me
look down and see
see me in a sea
of green, of blades of grass, so green
in the midst is me;

borne, you lift
and borne, you veer
by that which fills your soul
red and round
the wind directs

a place of rest untold;

the tree, beware
the tree right there
should finger pierce your skin
and dissipate
you back to where
before your life begins;

a cry I hear
a child is near
young mother bereft of son
"there, there,"
a voice beside her says,
"we'll get another one;"

you go, you go
you go, you go
fluttering string unseen;

freedom red
and round above
carried aloft so sweet;

The Beautiful Octopus

Arms of gold,
candelabra'd I am,
tips of light
with wicks bright,
unsnuffed, I give,
snuffed, I still gleam;

You see me
and admire my crafter,
but only for a moment
because you return
back to me
for who I am
and what I give;

No nettle to prick
nor ink of stink,
ugliness of mouth is gone,
fear of clutch and capture and drag and drown

9

all gone as well,
and my depths near hell
have been replaced
as you see me
hanging near heaven;

Behold!
crusted rust comes,
and the thought of things lost appears with it,
polish finds them again
somehow,
or at least
it feels that way,
and comfort returns,
so, tend to me
and be happy;

Yes, I once was made,
but that beginning
seems to walk backward,
further away,
until it disappears;

My end?
is there one?
who cares?
for you will always see me tomorrow;

The Tumbler

Poor tumbler,
Scorned for the living liquid spirits poured into you:
browned amber, poisoned honey, soured rose

Which deceive and hurt and cause regret:

 turning the peace of night's end into the curse of
 day's beginning,
 guiding quilled ink and note to mountaintop
 but ending in the mossy groans of tombs;
 admired for sturdy smoothness,
 yet your unshattering shatters many,
 and feet cut by your shards would be happier
 than eyes that see you filled again;

Gun blamed by hand, check accused by fraud,
Barabbas walks free again,
your innocence overlooked;

O' Tumbler!
the great oak's workmate!
citizen of many places!
remember and reckon your goodness!
at home with urn on mantel,
included with books on shelf,
and at rest on rested knee,
your heaviness befriends a man's hand;

you've joined lovers on lofty terrace,
heard secrets whispered in cellars,
sang with hunters on truck bed,
and sat in distant grass as sundown's prism;

consider the esteem of your kind,
treasured by potter,
favored by kings,
and quested by knights;

Keats wrote of your brother,
Keith sang of your sister,
winners embrace your mother,
and your father was at Gethsemane;

And of him,
The warrior psalmed:

"Blessed is the cup of God's wrath,
who else embanked its rivers?
or shorelined its oceans?
and had it not been held within,
wouldn't righteous anger have flooded us from the
beginning?
did purposeful creation not rest at its base?
did hope not extend up its stem?
did God's justice not wait at its brim?
perched there with unknowable patience?
did forgiveness not curve from its sides?
and does it not curve toward you?
Holy is the Lord, and merciful is His cup...
of which abundant life is promised."

The Prince Who
Ate No Grapes

silver trays
with sunlit rays
beaming off them bright,
chamber wisped in solitude,
await,
await for night;

and on them bounty lies,
colors, shapes, all seen,
but over all
a tainted pall,
a creeping plague of green:

the grapes!
the prince grimaced,

"Oh, that my aghast would shrivel the vines that
bore them!

Oh, that the axe of brutal judgement would fall in the
marketplace!
Oh, that the fair hands divinely commissioned for
selection and arrangement
would weep before priests!

my fruit,
my children,
so ruefully ruined at final garnish;

those grapes!
leprous blanket!
ovate stares seeing not,
attached to wooden nerve,
they look about before me
with privilege unearned;"
"Close!" I shout!
"Close!" I shout!
"Lest I pluck you out!
slither off my delicacy
and into fire's mouth!

my poms, my nans, my berries black,
apples red of sweet,

orange, kiwi, strawb, and plum,
the sight of passions heat,
my yearn of fondled touch,
and dainty, painless peel,
bite with rapture savored,
reclined at heaven's feet;

But nay!
green vultures!
over my thrill they hover!
eggs of pigeons a'fouled!
unswept pebbles in the monastery!

where are the minstrels,
to squish you under dance?

where are those who joust,
to pierce you with their lance?

and where are they?
who bow with 'sire'
and serve with 'liege,'
who hail with 'long live'

and breathe my name with the same breath of my
father's greatness?

and yet,
they bring your tormenting presence to me every day;

is this the life of a prince?
of a king to be?
always given splendor
but with prick of nettle teased?

Oh, destiny!
Oh, supremacy!
Oh, how you share your bed a'tryst with misery!"

the prince rose,
about the room,
he walked and circled twice,
he spied the grapes, he turned again,
the other direction thrice,
to window came,
he looked through pane,
his father's kingdom 'spansed,
towers, moat, and noble spires,

Babel in his hands;

but beyond he saw
fields and hills,
secretly desired,
things the king

did not know,
things in prince aspired;

green were the fields of solace,
the serenity he wished to know,
the green and round unventured hills
were where he wished to go;

grapes, more grapes!
upon those silver trays,
grapes, more grapes!
with lovely fruit arranged,
grapes, more grapes!
happy is the king,
grapes, more grapes!
a silent dirge he sings;

A Poem For Lisa
Who Never Was

and never will be

Happy Sneezes

we pranced and blew,
then danced in dew;
A-choo!...A-choo!...A-choo!

we whooshed and whisked,
with whispers we wished;
A-chish!...A-chish!...A-chish!

hand holds hand,
eyesight connects,
we beg of time,
remain at rest,
"Ka-choo!" sang the walrus
"cha-choo!" went the train
"the spell go'n git-choo,"
said Madame Thelisaint;

of breaths we launch forward
on cloverly toe,

21

skirt billow billow,
with wind we go;

and that which we left
in air-stirred surreal
gives chase to our feet
and seizes our heels!

Hah!...Chooh!

When A Man Lends His Land

I gave my friend an ear of corn from the rustling
ocean green,
he smiled at me,
I smiled at the sea,
it liked what it had seen;

he brought it home to his wife, and she blessed its
yellow fruit,
she held it up,
sent thanks above,
and cooked it with seasoned root;

the children took its silky strands, running down the
dusty road,
the man next door
was often poor,
but now his pipe overflowed;

the man came over the grassy hill, I smiled as
he neared,
he got down on one knee
and threw into the sea
ashes
as gray as his beard;

Love And Fate

where does fate come from,
and where does it go?
does love know?
does love know?

what welcomes it?
does wind hasten it?
does love know?
does love know?

it never hunts, but all things are prey,
it is never quested, but everything finds it;

soldiers die in its arms,
cowards cry to its face,
towers brace against it,
and moles burrow under it
but end up in its lair,
somewhere down there;

it brandishes against he who brandishes,
and he who flees in fear finds no asylum from it,
great stone walls topple at its siege,
and the blind shield their sightless gaze from it;

fate knows itself,
and love knows it knows itself:

but love gives itself,
it lowers itself,
it resigns itself,
and it sacrifices
because love knows itself too

it surrenders
on ugly altar
as its foe stands impotent beside her,

stained iron
and gloomy sky
bring death down quickly,

and love gasps
because it hurts

and gasps again because it has to hurt;

it gasps its last,
and then it gasps its first
as fate watches love validate itself,
consecrate itself,
and establish itself
as a living thing never lost;

what song can be sung of love?
what harp string can play its notes?
what feast can be set before its celebration?
even the eyes of Jupiter marvel
for love is greater than all that it contains;

and what it contains
is for the hand that trembles to take,
is for the soul that quakes to breathe in,
and is life for the fated to rejoice in,
it is
for you

Klaus & Clyde

"Mann kommt und mann stehen."
"Like a puffa smoke, he's there, he's faydin."

"Ein kampf fur Gott, bist du horen?
"Love'll give one comfort 'n curin'."

"Zerstoren nicht warden, al simmer leben."
"Seems y'need more heart re-shapin'."

"Gute seele hat den Deutshmann."
"S'there annyone humble in Munich or Bonn?"

"Halz mal yankee, ich gehe jetz kirche."
"Seems only fittin' t' complete the circle."

Dusk, Somewhere

ssh, my love, ssh
of tender age a'quiver

for that which comes
uncounted sums
of painful thrill delivered

relax, my love, yet don't relax
for tension has its joy

feel them both
and of them doth
hear vision without noise

down, my love, yes down, my love
for that is just and right

exposing where
your flesh most fair

bathes alone in light

ssh, my love, ssh my love
a kiss upon your face

have for now my tenderness
which in a moment fades

the chill, my love, the chill I see
ripple on your hills

bereft of ice
air sufficed
like mornings open sill

it's time, my love, it's time, my love
slip beneath the sea

as firmament
without relent
watches you hide
unseen

Faith: An Inferior Tapestry

nobody can see it clearly,
and yet, everyone sees something;

it's not what they thought it would be,
and someday it will be gone,
death follows it somewhere;

it's woven in the minds of those who saw it,
who stared at it,
who lay awake thinking about it
and dared to ask God about it;

if it hung on a wall,
it would look like burlap,
held there by tacks that occasionally fall out,
but it remains
because truth has mashed the threads of fabric into
the surface,
and if you jerk on it,

it will tear away,
but part of it will never come down;

it shows faded swirls of color,
finger painted by children?
brush strokes reserved for priests?
either? both?
does it matter?
if truth inspired it, shouldn't that be enough?

patches of mold reveal doubt,
but they can't be purified,
they are the tares of the fertile field;

fraying shows age,
but youthful strength can't be sewn in
because it hasn't been tempered over time;

it has holes of great tragedy
that can never be mended,
but even if they could,
it would never be the same,
a rebuilt city never forgets the fire that scorched
it long ago;

it is never mounted for all to see,
and when it isn't found, it's because it's been put away,
somewhere else,
and something else
has taken its place
until we long for it again,
seek for it again,
and find it again:

John The Baptist

…(A Quick Immersion)

born of barren womb,
embodying the great prophet returned from the dead,

an Aaronite,
following the anointed call of the Nazirite;

the son of a temple official,
a wilderness prodigal,
his voice proclaimed the new pilgrimage,
and signaled the dawn of deliverance;

clad in the skin of filthy beast,
he washed men clean in silty river banks;

imprisoned by bars
and doubt,
he was called the greatest ever born;

he swallowed the locust that plagued
and savored the honey of the promised land
with the same mouth;

he was not the king but ushered to throne;
he was not the sacrifice but identified the Lamb;
he was not the Love but beheld the dove;
and he was not the Glory
but presented
the One
who was;

Nostrildamnus

The curve,
the curl,
ticklish poke,
painful pluck;

Will she be mine tonight?
or waltz with another?
for one dead fly
must be uglier than the other,
even though the ointment that holds both
is unchanged by either;

Will we enter discussed joy?
sing with cheery fairies and happy ogres?
and ice skate on beams from Neptune?
will we smell blue?
taste rose?
laugh on cantering horseback under umbrellas of elm?

or will my stray hairs appear as glaring dots
in Sunday Afternoon on the Isle of Grand Jutta?

They must go,
specifically that one;
Ahhh…cold steel of pinch,
go back in
and spare nothing;

Where Light And Heat Meet

The sun was over here,
Infernally white!

And over there,
iron girders sagged and sank
with a molten clank
as the sun whispered to them;

How have I survived between them?
my breath still has air,
why does my skin feel cool?
could a flower grow at my feet?

If a bird flew backwards,
could I ask why?
should the empty noose explain itself?
and if I live now,
only to die a minute later,
have I not seen the compassion of God?

this is where light and heat meet,
this is where mercy lies;

Discontented Man Blues

I'm sick of oatmeal,
and I'm sick of my shoes,
tired of waking up late
and surfing Yahoo news;

If I had tickets to Bali
or even to Cali,
I'd be on the plane,
wishing I'd taken a train;

because time, time, time…
on my hands
is heavy like sand,
oh, yes, it is;

I got a big purpose,
a surplus of purpose,
but tick tock of clock
turns purpose into porpoise;

it's like turquoise
on an Iroquois,
it doesn't change his skin to blue;

and even if I loved oatmeal,
I'd still be sick of my shoes;

Green Grass In An Empty Room

In the corner of my soul
is where I am;

walls extend outward
and I see another corner of myself,
directly across from myself,
but it is one
that I can never go to;

I imagine great trees there,
but their leaves fall with the weight of iron;

I see wonderful palms in fluttering shade
and pools of precious blue,
but under their pristine depths
lie the carcasses of dreams,
fossilized by falsehood;

42

and if I could go there,
what would await me
is the view across from it,
which is where I am now;

that corner of the soul sees
splendor overlooked,
gratitude forgotten,
hope warehoused in cardboard boxes;

and it says,
"Arise, fortunate one!
forsake your bed, which welcomes nothingness
and nurtures the friendship of sleep,
for where you are is where you want to be,
and what you want is what you already have;

let he who governs scales reveal the measure of your
substance,
let his gavel render your spirit fulfilled,
and let his great horn proclaim victory;

sing of things unseen yet known
and guard the gold of truth,
redeem your wasted weariness,
rest as one renewed:"

Ode To E Tenebris

is that it, my friend?
my dead friend,
my dead friend I've read?

read and wished
for scrawl in view,
etched anew,
the thing from you unsaid?

hope groped
and peace on leash,
hungry destiny fed?

or should I search for treasure still, by myself unled?

Oh, how I longed
for the honesty of your pen to finally say it!

gold on pulp,
portrait dusted off,
a whisper scales Everest,
and a single wet tear brings cleansing;

has it come at last?
Please! be so
Please! be so

Let your essays shrink before its height,
Algernon agrees,
Endymion abreeze,
Profundis leaves his chains,
the ghost sleeps in Canterville,
a rose's petal stains,
the millionaire feasts in tattered rags,
WH tells his name,
your mentor cries, "Paradisio!" from high above
the flames;

is that it, my friend?
Please! let it be so
Please! let it be so

The Wishing Well

in the agora,
where sons laid stones
that their fathers named plaza, moat, and arch;

a fountain pool,
surrounded by the scurry of crowding feet,
stands tall in its shortness;

and down through blue and marbled clear,
we see them,
the faces of the famous,
looking back at us
in stoic periphery;

we remember them that way
because we see them that way
everyday;

and they see us up here,
as if through ice,
obscurely clear;
the sound of spray,
we hear it like rain from above,
they hear it like thunder from below;

the sound of coins tossed in,
we hear them *bloop* from above,
they hear them *blawp* from below;

many of us request healing,
others request lovers,

some make childish pleas,
some make agnostic prayers,
and some can't help themselves in being prop-
erly pious;

we ask for:
toys
the perfect pie crust
the lottery
an A+

less gray
hamburgers
an OSU victory
quiet
the weekend to last forever
Maureen?...tonight?
an orange velvet sunset
for someone to…just. shut. up...for once

and they see us up here,
with chatter,
with boredom,
with awe displaced,
a kaleidoscope of hopes;

yet,
sometimes,
there is an, "I wish,"
and a *kerplunk*
that is refreshingly new,
it startles everything else,
above and below;

it splashes in
and embraces before sinking;

and then it begins the sweetness of glide:
to one side,
where it angles up
and starts its traverse,
racing to the other side of its domain;

its west becomes its east,
and then its east becomes its west,
and then it soars across again;

borne on crests unseen,
loft without air,
it neither navigates
nor is navigated;

the jellyfish,
the frisbee,
the pendulum,
it is somehow all three,
and it owns the ocean it is in;

they watch it from below,
and we watch it from above,
wishing,
wishing we could behold its majestic descent forever,
and for three seconds,
the fear of eternity leaves us;

the wish settles,
and wherever it settles is where it was supposed
to settle,
virtue has its own throne
and is honored wherever it is;

this wish
snared us at one moment
and seized us for another
and made itself lovelier than anything imaginable;

it was the wish unwished,
the wish that subdued self,
it was the wish given
for someone else:

The Two Masks

Agony,
it is I,
Ecstasy,
your cruel mate,
the counterpart that completes you;

I am bliss,
as far as anything can be from you,
yet now near to you,
here with you,
a friendship of clouds and molten iron;

was your wait for me never-ending?
did vanity fill you?
did it lodge in your woeful countenance?
do you see elation elevated in mine?

as the sweetness of large brown plums are too high for
your hands,

and the nest in the crook of the tall tree teases you
with rest,
it pleases me
that what you desire you will never have;

behold yourself
on great hills of snow,
where coldness burns skin
and the valley between is where I am,
down deep,
where flowers of musk caress
and grotto gives solace,
from there I call to you,
hidden from view,
hidden from you;

weep not,
or weep!
for I am unchanged;

ache for,
quake for,
break for,
for you are Agony;

but know this…my unloved lover,
I need you;

for without darkness, who can perceive light?
how is goodness justified without the conten-
tion of evil?
and how is life fully appreciated without under-
standing it could end?

you are still Agony,
and I am still Ecstasy,
and together,
the tragedy written for many
is who we are

Photograph Of A Foggy Path
Into The Woods

Winding into whiteness
is what we see,
it's what we want,
and what we fear;

it is welcomely wide…for the prudent and the naïve,
paved for safety…but is it safe beyond what we see?
reception line?…or gauntlet
procession to banquet?…or predation
do trees harbor haven for songbirds?…or ghosts
if we hear the footsteps are they of kings?…or thieves
do they sound different from our own?

but from where we are,
we love it for what it is,
even the mystery of where it goes,
and that is enough;

Photo Of A Thorn Cluster

It was there we saw the great plague of generations
who chose to be blind and stumble into wretchedness,
rather than walk the bright streets of love;

spikes so cruel
and so many in number
that a mere glance
warns aloud in mercy;

does the bee not forsake your sweetness?
does the spider not spin elsewhere?
even the vultures avoid your dead;

no siren lures to your fatal reefs,
no scent brings hounds to your lair,
but the whisper of foolishness
and selfishness of self
shun the scrolls of wisdom
and dare your promise of pain;

impalement of one,
mere prick of another,
they both return to your altar
and in sickness
sacrifice others on frigid slabs
in the depths of needled misery;

Photo Of A Skyline

my Canaan,
the place of promise;
the path of pearl rolls toward her
and ends at the feet of her throne;

shall I look back?
no, for the journey is already forgotten,
shall I race ahead?
no, for the splendor of the city slows the pace of time
and the moment of destiny
triumphs in itself;
shall I sing with the lamps of amber?
shall I whisper through the great lattice of the span?
shall I wave my hand across the heights of stones?
indeed, I will, for her gates are open;

and as I walk toward her,
she says,
"come join me
for our wait is over."

Photo Of A Storm Cloud

turbulent tempest,
tufts of green reach for you,
they welcome your groans and your tears,
while others marvel at your thoughts;

but a black roil churns unseen,
seizing the peace of timid marshes
and chaffing brittle hills scorched by drought,
without wind to wave its darkness away;

Photograph Under A Bridge

and the guide in white
led me down
to where I heard the thunder of progress above
and saw the brilliance of steel shoulders,
woven by the might of men,
resting on stone backbone
of great formidable girth,
while the unfathomable wonder of the river
swept undaunted beneath it all.

Saad's Saga

a child was found in an alleyway,
many thought he'd die that very day,
but he lived and donned a pair of gloves
and fought in the city of Brotherly Love;

his birthplace was a battle zone
that toughs and scruffs somehow call home,
air filled with smoke and police sirens,
broken glass where there should be dandelions;

to live, a child must learn other ways,
no eating from silver spoons or trays,
don't wince at pain or cry over sorrow,
you'll trip over today if you dream of tomorrow;

as the boy grew up, he learned one thing,
to replace the streets with ropes and a ring,
a microcosm of the world he knew,
you'll die if you don't beat a face black and blue;

finally, he fought for the title,
the champ, a horse no one could bridle,
the two waged war with sweat and blood,
to win was to swim against raging flood;

he took the belt and gained great fame
by beating all and changing his name,
but the day came when he could take no more,
like the old hinge of an ever-slamming door;

"What shall I do?" he started to cry
and looked up to the heavenly sky,
"My body is beaten, my soul is torn,
this struggle is just like the day I was born."

Waiting For Regret

the thing thrown
breeds regret,
bleeds remorse,
and bids one to beg;

carelessness lobbed,
thoughtlessness tossed,
a wish,
then a vow
from a heart now at loss;

arc rises from below,
ascending above,
trajectory sometime,
sometime, will come;

for nine days watched
by air-given clock,
nine days await
for descent from thereof;

the wait,
the awful wait,
tumult unheard,
chaos unseen,
will dawn sing with birds?

will loudness land?
will hope hide in trees?
when silence moans out
with dread finally freed?

can crooked be straightened?
brokenness healed?
fix-up of mess-up?
stained become clean?

the wait,
the awful wait

 # Seattle

rains electric wish
frees tomorrow's windy traffic,
and spike of lonely steel
embraces clouds that never left;

once,
a giant awoke
and spat burning locusts from his belly,

and once,
shouts mingled with broken glass,
as faithful and frolic stood together,

and once,
waves brought awful relics from a long highway,
and once,
a terrible decision haunted the applause of your
gladiators;

but you are beautiful, still:

the great bean,
the great bird,
the four great children,
and the queen of all spiders,
they are yours;

those who leave you
never seem to get over you;

and those who come back to you
never want to leave again;

and where you are,
I want to be again,
but where I am now
is where I remember you
because away from you
the memory of you
is never forgotten:

The Frog

frog upon a lily pad,
looking into space,
eating flies and croaking,
thinking of this place;

I live in water dark and green,
but yet, I need the air,
which of them do I need most?
why do I even care?

does my ripple touch the shore?
do my squeaks resound?
does fear of snake or yearn for bug
become my only crown?

was pharaoh's curse my legacy?
does karma hold me dear?
and if I am a fabled prince,
does kiss change how I appear?

frog upon a lily pad,
staring into space,
eating flies and croaking,
thinking of this place;

and why do they say I taste like chicken?

The Second Sickness

we became ill
waiting for illness,
it could kill us,
what followed could kill us too;

for fear of the first
made us afraid of things worse;

so, we lived,
waiting for the first,
immersed in the second;

flood waters of poverty,
boredom,
and isolation
became the air we breathed;

and we wondered which sickness was worse,
we said the first

and secretly thought the second;

don't touch,
don't get too close,
don't look?

don't talk?
there's nothing to talk about,
except sickness;

would it find our door?
should we seal with Passover blood?
the heart still leaks;

should we handle sackcloth?
or purify ash anew?

and where do we go?
if we are confined to ourselves
in the second sickness;

above!
the paraclete!
the lovely one on tireless wings!

ANDY HAWK

he watches you,
he swoops down for you

She Whom I Behold

I know a woman beautiful,
her face is like the sun,
her golden rays warm my days,
in evening, she is gone;

a rainbow is her loving arms,
as pretty as her face,
when rain weeps down, she soothes my world,
yet we cannot embrace;

the sweet earth is her body,
its fruit is of her womb,
I know she dies in winter,
but I only see her bloom;

for her heart is from the Father,
which I can surely see,
and it is He who lets her be
so beautiful to me;

Stone Vs Ice

Which of ye
is greater, see?
for both of ye
seem same to me;

"It is I," says I, "great in count,
tiny grain, majestic mount,
I am of old and have no age,
from me come things that wars are waged;"

"It's me," says me, "above, below,
skin of frost, immense in floe,
I, too, am old and have no years,
I cap your poles, your seas I rear;"

"Still I," says I, "was first I came
for after null and void was made;"

"Yet me," says me, "was before thee,

 by three, deployed, in canopy;"

"I'm unmoved," says I,
"I cover you in winter," says me
"my sun melts you," says I
"my liquid sister erodes you," says me
"I never disappear," says I
"I always come back," says me

"I have songs written about me," says I
"me too," says me

"Solid...solid as a—-"
"ICE ICE BABY...da dumdumdum dada dumdum"
"I am a rock...I am—"
"COLD...AS...I-I-I-CE...you—"
"Rock of ages...clef—"
"Fire 'n ice...fire 'n ice...you—"

Of Flowers Affaired

Today's garden
appeared before,
and of it then,
we now search for;

But youthful eyes
saw other blooms,
of them we selected
on choice afternoon;

Care and ground,
ground and care,
toil and soil,
'til winter laid bare;

Years became questions,
minutes had fears,
in hours that passed
as April neared;

Hope became helpless, we worked nonetheless,
the moon ascended with Spring's duress;

so we worked and looked,
and we spied, and we spent,
we thought things we shouldn't
and dreamed to repent,
we made things of nothing
and watered them too,
'til they grew into something
both true and untrue,
with one eye we gazed,
the other stayed firm,
'til vision was cross-eyed
and blinded by germ,
like Israel to eagle
on treetop of pine,
regal and royal
but roots undivine,
a garden of fancy
with blooms of the mind
became what we wanted
while the real sat behind;

ANDY HAWK

We see larger petal and absence of thorn,
We forget about winter and death that is born;

for all gardens seem lovely,
and this one seems pure,
the rose of today
is how we are lured;

Lullaby

awake and await,
the hour of owls summons itself
in outer blankness,
where dreams hatch in the arms of trees
and stare through crookedness into windows;

I see them,
stealing from stars
and making unreal shapes
that cause pursuit
and threaten impact
and suggest plummet
from places known and unknown alike;

clouds of razor wire,
wicked operas,
the stench of sick rain,
and fruit with sharp teeth
invisibly appear from dark corners

where I lay alone;
I hear the whisper that reminds me
that without light,
shadows don't exist at all,
and the moon
is merely a dead mirror of the living sun,
which still gives life,
even at night;

let heaviness sink into floor
as He who loves you bears you up,
let sharpness shrink to dull edge as He lifts you out,
let sigh bridge to sigh
as you feel the blanket of His breath,
and the peace He loves to give you,
sleep in His cradled warmth,
sleep

CPSIA information can be obtained
at www.ICGtesting.com
Printed in the USA
BVHW041732141220
595676BV00013BA/2112